I Am the Greatest

Other Books by Karl Evanzz

The Messenger:
The Rise and Fall of Elijah Muhammad

The Judas Factor: The Plot to Kill Malcolm X

I Am the Greatest

—◆◆◆—

*The Best Quotations
from Muhammad Ali*

Compiled by Karl Evanzz

**Andrews McMeel
Publishing**

Kansas City

02 03 04 05 06 QUF 10 9 8 7 6 5 4 3 2 1

Library of Congress Cataloging-in-Publication Data
Ali, Muhammad, 1942–
   I am the greatest : the best quotations from Muhammad Ali / compiled by Karl Evanzz.
        p. cm.
Includes bibliographical references.
    ISBN 0-7407-2226-3
   1. Ali, Muhammad, 1942—Quotations. 2. Boxers (Sports)—United States—Quotations. I. Evanzz, Karl. II. Title.
    GV1132.A44 A36 2002
    796.83'092—dc21

                                        2001053402

The quotations is this publication were compiled by the editor and were not provided personally by Muhammad Ali. Quotations were compiled from various sources including published media reports.

*For Everyday
Heroes and Heroines*

Introduction: For Want of a Bike

The first of Odessa and Cassius Marcellus Clay's two children, Cassius Clay Jr., was born on January 17, 1942. Another son, Rudolph Clay, was born two years later in September. Odessa Clay made a living as a domestic helper, while Cassius Sr. painted billboards and signs around their hometown of Louisville, Kentucky, and neighboring locales. The parents nicknamed their baby "GG" because he made that sound when they played with him as he lay in his crib. (Ali later joked that what he was really trying to say was "Golden Gloves.")

Clay Jr. lived a relatively uneventful life until he was twelve years old. In the summer of 1954, the theft of his prized bicycle changed the course of his life. Clay surveyed the neighborhood for the bike, crying and threatening to break the offending hand. Friends advised him to go see Joe Martin, a black police officer who taught boxing at a local gymnasium. After Clay cautioned Martin to apprehend the thief before he took justice into his own hands, Martin suggested to Clay that he learn how to fight before actually getting into one. Enthralled by the artistry and mathematical approach to pugilism displayed by the youngsters in the gym, Clay soon forgot about the bike and began focusing on another prize — prizefighting. The ninety-pound youth trained tirelessly under Martin at the Columbia Gymnasium for the next three years. Before his thirteenth birthday, Clay had his first of many appearances on a locally televised boxing show produced by Martin. The show was aptly named *Tomorrow's Champions*.

Clay was already a local hero by the time he entered Louisville's Central High School at age fifteen. Media attention began in September 1957 with a three-paragraph story in the *Louisville Courier-Journal* acknowledging his extraordinary boxing abilities. In December 1957 Clay traveled to Cincinnati for the National Golden Gloves championship, his first of many successive and successful appearances. He lost fewer than a dozen fights over the next three years and quickly earned national recognition as one of the best amateur boxers in the nation. He easily earned a spot on the American boxing team for the 1960 Olympic Games in Rome, Italy.

In September 1960, Clay won a gold medal at the Olympics in Rome. On his flight home, he prepared a poem that he read before a small group of supporters at the airport:

How Cassius Clay Took Rome

To make America the greatest is my goal
So I beat the Russian, and I beat the Pole
And for the USA won the Medal of Gold
Italians said, "You're greater than Cassius of Old
We like your name, we like your game
So make Rome your home if you will."
I said, "I appreciate your kind hospitality.
But the USA is my country still
Cause they waiting to welcome me in Louisville."

After receiving the backing of a group of Louisville businessmen who dubbed the up-and-coming contender the "Louisville Lip" because he bragged incessantly about his pugilistic skills, Clay developed public relations ploys that quickly led from local to national and international fame.

Following Archie Moore, a black boxer who used clever advertising gimmicks to coax Rocky Marciano into a title fight, Clay spent two years taunting Sonny Liston. In late 1963, Liston's managers finally relented, realizing that the fight, which they felt certain Liston would win, would generate millions in ticket sales. People were anxious to see someone, anyone, burst the Louisville Lip's lips and in doing so, stop his relentless bragging. Alas, Clay's game plan paid off. On February 25, 1964, Liston stepped into the ring with Clay at Madison Square Garden. Seven rounds later, Clay stepped out of the ring and into history as the new heavyweight boxing champion of the world.

But Clay did not live happily ever after. In fact, he was embroiled in the most damaging controversy of his career less than twenty-four hours later. On February 26, Clay stood before a horde of reporters and admitted that he was a member of the controversial black separatist sect called the Nation of Islam, or Black Muslims. The admission was deeply troubling for most Americans because Clay was standing next to Malcolm X, then among the most reviled and feared black men in the world, when he made the announcement. Making matters worse, Clay concurrently announced that he was rejecting his Christian name and taking an Islamic name: Muhammad Ali.

Battle lines were quickly drawn around Ali by the media, the military, and men who controlled professional boxing.

On February 27, the day after the admission, a U.S. Army spokesman told reporters that Ali would be drafted in quick order. Members of Congress and of boxing commissions called press conferences to denounce Ali as "morally unfit" to hold boxing's championship belt because racism and anti-Americanism was implicit in his Black Muslim membership; as such, he was a bad symbol for American youth. And sports writers refused to acknowledge the boxer's new name; they insisted upon calling him Cassius Clay over his repeated protests.

Ali's reaction to the Army's decision to draft him was as quick as it was unexpected. He would not fight for his country, Ali said, and was willing to go to jail but never to war.

"You want me to do what the white man says and go fight a war against some people I don't know nothing about [and] get some freedom for some other people when my own people can't get theirs here?" he asked rhetorically.

He would have none of that, Ali said repeatedly in interviews over the next several months.

As the American people broke into two main camps over the morality of the war in Vietnam— those over thirty on one side and those under thirty on the side opposing the war—powerful government officials set in motion a plan to yank Ali out of his boxing trunks and drop him into an Army uniform. Before the title fight that nearly everyone thought he would lose, Ali was classified by the U.S. Army as 1Y, meaning that he was intellectually unqualified to serve. But due to heavy battlefield losses in Vietnam, the Army in late 1965 lowered the passing score on its intelligence measuring test to 15. In February 1966 Ali learned that not only was he now eligible to serve but that under his new status as a 1A draftee candidate, he probably would be drafted within the next thirty days.

Ali declared that he would not fight in Vietnam or in any war waged by the American government. When he officially refused to be inducted on April 28, 1967, he was immediately stripped of his boxing title and banned from fighting in his own country and in most of the western world. He was indicted on May 8 for refusing induction and was convicted one month later in a Houston courtroom. He was fined $10,000 and given a five-year prison term.

Ali's career spiraled downward as he remained free on bond pending appeal. The appellate process was long and costly, and Ali found it difficult to make it financially. His inability to make a living the only way he knew how was devastating for the boxer. He had to borrow pennies from friends to buy gasoline and accept meals from strangers who admired him. But no matter how bad things got, Ali always believed in himself. "Allah okays the adversary to try us," he told reporters during an extended stay in Africa in 1966. "That's how he sees if you're a true believer."

To earn money, he signed a contract to stage a computer-generated "boxing match" with Rocky Marciano. Predictably, the owners of the virtual match, shown on movie screens throughout the country, decided that Marciano would defeat Ali.

Like many African Americans, Ali suspected that the whole draft episode was a red herring for a government angry about his membership in a controversial religious group, and he believed that the government was out to destroy him financially and as a man. He was correct on both counts. His three-year legal battle with the Goliath of governments ended much the same as the original, with Goliath beheaded and with this modern-day David marching triumphantly into history and legend. During his trial, FBI agents testified that they had monitored telephone calls to which Ali was a party and that physical surveillance of his activities made it possible for the government to exert some control over his fate. The Supreme Court ultimately accepted Ali's appeal. On June 28, 1971, the Court reversed Ali's conviction. One month later, Ali was back in the ring after a nearly four-year layoff. The decision affirmed something Ali already knew: No man can control the fate of another forever.

In standing up to the system against the Vietnam War, a war most teenagers believed was morally wrong, Ali became a folk hero not only to young African Americans but also to young white Americans who were struggling with their consciences about the moral justification for the war.

And in taking an unpopular stance on one of the most contentious political issues of the 1960s, Ali lost three of his most promising years as an athlete to court fights. But he held on to and gained something far more important: his faith and the faith of his fellow men in him.

Today, at age sixty, Ali is the best-known person on the planet, according to any number of reputable public opinion polls. *The Guinness Book of World Records*, in listing Ali as the "most written-about human being who ever lived," placed him ahead of Lincoln, Jesus, and Napoleon. And to think that this hero who everyone knows might never have been were it not for a thief—the first of his many adversaries—whom no one knows.

The Best Quotations

Africa

I haven't been home in 410 years. I'm going there to see what home looks like.

—The Washington Post, May 17, 1964
Ali's comment as he checked his passport
prior to his first trip to Africa in May 1964.
Elijah Muhammad taught the boxer and
his fellow Black Muslims that slavery
began in the Americas in 1555.

African-American Music

The funny thing I find is that everywhere I go they're crazy about soul music. I hear James Brown, the Jackson Five, and the Supremes over here [in Europe] . . . when these people come on, the whole world starts dancing. They all follow the American Negro. I didn't know that until I started traveling.

—*The Washington Post,* *July 19, 1972*

Aging

I've punched and been punched since I was twelve, and it seems like every time I fight lately, something gets hurt.

—A very weary Ali after winning a split decision over Ken Norton in Los Angeles on September 11, 1973

Ali Shuffle

It's something that will go down in history, like the left hook.

*—**The Washington Post**, November 15, 1966*

It was just a publicity stunt to start with, but I'm going to keep it in my act. It helped me get out of the corners.

*—**The Washington Post**, November 16, 1966*
Explaining how the Ali Shuffle was born

Amateur

I'm the amateur light-heavyweight champion of the world, and I don't have a penny.

—*Newsweek* *magazine, September 19, 1960*
Reflecting on why he was anxious
to turn professional

America

There's no place like home, especially when home is America.

—Upon returning from a five-nation tour of Africa, February 10, 1980

Archie Moore

■ ■ ■ I liked his style in the ring and especially out of it. I remembered the way Archie gained a title shot from Marciano by using colorful gimmicks that forced Rocky to respond. He had run ads in newspapers with a picture of Marciano in convict clothes and a headline that read: "One hundred thousand dollar reward for anybody who can get Marciano into a ring with Sheriff Archie Moore."

—*The Greatest: My Own Story*

Attractiveness

I'm so pretty that I can hardly stand to look at myself!

——◆◆◆——

I'm as pretty as a girl.

—Prefight bragging in late 1963
before his first battle with
Sonny "the Bear" Liston

The Beatles

All races love the Beatles. I love the music. I used to train to their music.

—◆◆◆—

I hope to impress them with the idea that this is money to help people all over the world.

> —*The Washington Post,* January 16, 1977
> Ali made a vain attempt to reunite the
> Beatles in a concert for the benefit of the
> poor children of the world. He thought
> the concert would generate the first of
> $200 million to establish a permanent
> international relief agency.

Boxer's Hands

A fighter's only weapons are his hands.
If they go, he goes.

—*The Greatest: My Own Story*

Boxing Commissioners

They're expecting me to come back looking fat, looking bad. They think they've done me in. But I'm going to fool them.

*— **Life** magazine, October 23, 1970*

Boxing Opponents

If anybody ever dreamed of [knocking me down], he'd wake up and apologize.

— *Life* magazine, July 9, 1971

Boxing Prowess

Now, a whole lot of people ain't going to like this, but I'm going to tell you the truth—you asked me. It's too many great old fighters to go listing them one by one. But ain't no need to. I think that Joe Louis, in his prime, could have whipped them all—I mean anyone you want me to name. And I would have beat Louis.

Look, it ain't never been another fighter like me. Ain't never been no nothing like me.

—*Playboy* magazine, September 1964

I float like a butterfly and sting like a bee.

—*The Washington Post*, February 24, 1964

When I fight Liston, I'm going to have five of the prettiest girls in the world in my corner. I'll have one to take off my crown, one to handle my robe, another to spray the corners of the ring with perfume, one to give me a pat on the back, and another to comb my hair.

—*The Washington Post*, November 15, 1963

15

I'm the unrevealed champion. I'm the only fighter who predicts the exact round in which my opponent will fall. I am the greatest.

—*The Washington Post,* October 14, 1962

Did you ever see such a graceful man?

—*Ali's query to reporters while watching a film of his first-round defeat of Liston in May 1965*

You stand a better chance in Vietnam with a BB gun than you do with me.

—*The Washington Post,* June 24, 1972
*Warning to Bob Foster prior
to a match in Las Vegas*

Boxing Dangers

There was the smell of death in that ring tonight.

> —*The Washington Post,* May 15, 1977
> *After a torturous fight with Joe Frazier in*
> *Manila in October 1975, the so-called*
> *"Thrilla in Manila"*

Boxing is not as dangerous as football. If we stopped all the things that caused accidents, cars would be first. Hundreds of thousands die every year in America from having handguns in the house.

—Associated Press, May 14, 1985
Ali's reaction when asked about
a growing national campaign to ban
professional boxing

Boxing Shoes

I want the people to notice me and that's why I do all that fancy dancing in the ring before I start winning my fights. . . . I liked Galivan's white shoes [when he saw Kid Galivan fight on television] and I always knew that my boxing shoes would be white because people notice white shoes, especially if they are being worn on fancy feet.

—On the eve of his fight with Cleveland Williams in November 1966

Boxing Suspension

Sometimes I still wonder just how great I might have been if I could have fought all the time. But I still wouldn't change anything. The way things ended, it all made me better as far as history is concerned. I try not to worry about the past.

*—**The Washington Post,** July 8, 1979*
Reflecting on his nearly four-year-long
suspension from boxing

Brotherhood

All men are brothers—black, brown, red, or white. None of that devil stuff. We used to [believe] that at one time, but he [Wallace D. Mohammed] saved us from that.

—*The Washington Post,* July 5, 1984

Champions

Champions aren't made in gyms. Champions are made from something they have deep inside them—a desire, a dream, a vision. They have to have the skill and the will. But the will must be stronger than the skill.

—*The Greatest: My Own Story*

Charity

To be able to give away riches is mandatory if you wish to possess them. This is the only way to be truly rich.

—*PR Newswire,* September 25, 2000
*From a speech made before accepting the
Hannah Neil World of Children Award
in Columbus, Ohio*

Children

Children are refugees from heaven.

*—**Louisville** magazine, April 1, 2001*
Reflecting on his and Lonnie Ali's
decision to adopt a child

Contenders

The boy who's going to be Muhammad Ali is only about ten years old [today].

— *The Washington Post,* December 29, 1966

Daughters

People ask me how many children I have and I say one boy and seven mistakes.

◄◆►

I've bought a big long shotgun to give all the boys who come looking for my daughters.

—*Associated Press,* May 14, 1985
*Joking with reporters about the
gender of his children*

Determination

My name is Cassius Marcellus Clay. I'm the Golden Gloves champion of Louisville. I'm going to be the heavyweight champion of the world.

—*The Sun-Sentinel* (Fort Lauderdale), July 20, 1997
Ali's first words to Angelo Dundee when
they met in Louisville in 1957

Dignity

The only place they can take my title away from me is in the ring—and nobody can do it there, either.

—*The Washington Post,* September 15, 1964
Muhammad Ali's reply after the World
Boxing Association threatened to take his
newly earned heavyweight boxing title
for "conduct detrimental to boxing." The
conduct in question was Ali's admission on
February 26, 1964, that he was a member
of the Nation of Islam. Ali was stripped
of his title on September 14, the first time
in boxing history that a heavyweight
champion's title was revoked.

Diplomacy

I want to get out of boxing . . . put on a coat and tie and carry a briefcase and be the black Henry Kissinger.

—*The Washington Post,* April 17, 1976

Draft

I'm giving up my title, my wealth, and maybe my future. Many great men have been tested for their religious beliefs. If I pass this test, I'll come out stronger than ever.

—Sports Illustrated magazine, May 1967
Ali viewed the dilemma of the draft—to
go or not to go—as a test of his faith.

I'm happy because I'm free. I've made the stand all black people are gonna have to make sooner or later: whether or not they can stand up to the master.

—*Life* magazine, October 25, 1968

—◆—

Why should I drop bombs and bullets on brown people in Vietnam while so-called Negro people in Louisville are treated like dogs?

—*1967 press conference*

Draft Charges

Have Madison Square Garden send
all the judges ringside seats.
Let the judges in free,
courtesy of me,
Muhammad Ali.

*—**Newsweek** magazine, July 9, 1971
Commenting on an anticipated favorable
decision from Supreme Court on his
draft evasion appeal*

They did what they thought was right, and I did what I thought was right.

—*The Washington Post*, *June 29, 1971*
After the U.S. Supreme Court overturned
his draft-evasion conviction on June 28

Education

I would advise kids to go to school, get educated, and carry the briefcase. He who carries the briefcase ends up in the best shape.

—On whether he regretted
doing poorly in high school and
not going to college, July 13, 1971

Elijah Muhammad

Elijah is not teaching hate when he tells us about all the evil things the white man has done, any more than [whites are] teaching hate when you tell about what Hitler did to the Jews. That's not hate; that's history.

—The New York Times Magazine,
May 28, 1967

Elvis Presley

I'd like to be a singer like Elvis Presley.

—*The Chicago Daily News,* September 8, 1960
*Response to reporter who asked him what
he wanted to do after the Olympics*

Epiphany

The first time I felt truly spiritual in my life was when I walked into the [Nation of Islam's] temple in Miami.

—The Greatest: My Own Story

Equal Rights Amendment

Someone's got to wear the pants and some-one's got to wear the dress. There isn't going to be any equality. If you want to be equal with me, you can get your own Rolls Royce, your own house, and your own million dollars.

—*The Washington Post,* July 9, 1979

Faith

He [God] doesn't talk to me in a voice, not like [what one sees] on TV. It is more of a feeling, a sense of what I have to do. Whatever this is, I'm in tune with it.

> —*The Washington Post,* September 12, 1975
> *Explaining his relationship with God to*
> *reporters at his training camp*

Fame

I'm gonna talk and talk and talk, and all the world's gonna know my name.

—*Newsweek* magazine, March 19, 1963
*On his decision to use braggadocio
to make a name for himself*

Fans

I cannot shake everybody's hand. I cannot kiss everybody. There are too many Muslims in the world [for me to do so].

—The Washington Post, September 27, 1975
Pleading with Muslim fans inside a mosque
in Manila who had him "trapped" on the eve
of a fight with Joe Frazier

I love to be booed. They can boo me, yell at me, and throw peanuts at me as long as they pay to get in.

—*Newsweek* magazine, March 25, 1963

Fools

A wise man can act a fool, but a fool cannot act as a wise man.

———◈———

Why do I play the fool? Because . . . with some people you have to [play] the fool in order to be a friend.

—*The Washington Post,* March 20, 1976

Friends

Show me the company you keep and I'll tell you who you are.

—The Washington Post, March 20, 1976

He taught me a new punch—the "anchor punch." And that's the one I used to knock Liston out.

> —*When reporters realized that Lincoln Perry, one of the most reviled African Americans of the 1960s (he played Stepin Fetchit in many Shirley Temple movies), was in Miami with Ali, they wanted to know why the contender would associate with a man who represented the worst stereotypes of black people. Ali cleverly gave them an answer that had a double meaning: (1) They were stereotyping Perry, and (2) we ought to choose our friends not for who they appear to be on the outside but for who they are inside.*

> —**The Washington Post,** *February 28, 1964*

Good Deeds

Everything I do, I say to myself, "Will God accept this?"

—People magazine, January 13, 1997

Greatest

God gave me this physical impairment [Parkinson's disease] to remind me that I am not the greatest. He is.

—*The Washington Post,* *June 9, 1998*

Haile Selassie

If he had his picture taken with me, I thought it might do him some good.

—**The Washington Post,** October 15, 1963
Explaining why he called on Ethiopian
Emperor Haile Selassie while Selassie
was visiting a Philadelphia housing project

Happiness

I conquered the world, and it didn't bring me true happiness. The only true satisfaction comes from honoring and worshipping God.

—The Ottawa Citizen, July 14, 1991

Hate

I didn't hate. Not then; not now. What I was doing was like a doctor giving someone a needle and hurting them a little to kill an infection. In the end it helps.

—***Muhammad Ali in Perspective*** *by Thomas Hauser*
Ali explaining why he did not regret things
he said about white people in the months
following his admission in February 1964 that
he was a member of the Nation of Islam

Human Nature

Look for the good qualities and not the bad in everybody. There's a lot of good in the worst of us and a lot of bad in the best of us.

—*Business World,* *August 29, 2000*
From a lecture Ali gave before eight thousand
people at Ortanez University in Manila prior
to his fight with Joe Frazier in 1975

It's nature to run from something that runs after you. And it's nature to chase something that runs away from you.

—*The Washington Post,* March 20, 1976
On women and power in love relationships

Humor

Sometimes I laugh at what I do [harder] than anyone else.

—*Life* magazine, October 25, 1968

Idols

Sometimes I think too many people put me on a pedestal before and made me into an idol. And that's against [religion]; there are no idols in Islam. So maybe this problem I have is God's way of reminding me and everyone else about what's important.

—*The Ottawa Citizen, July 14, 1991*

Imagination

The man who has no imagination stands on the earth. He has no wings; he cannot fly. The Wright Brothers had imagination. Columbus had it when he said that the world was round. The man who said, "I'm going to the moon," had imagination. And so do I.

—*Newsweek* magazine, September 29, 1975

Intelligence

I didn't say I am the smartest. I said I am the greatest.

*—When asked to explain his low score on
his second predraft mental aptitude test,
March 20, 1964*

—◆◆◆—

For two years the government caused me international embarrassment, letting people think I was a nut. Sure, it bothered me, and my mother and father suffered. Now they jump up and make me 1A without even an official notification of a test. Why did they let me be considered a nut, an illiterate, for two years?

—*Ali's reaction when he learned from a reporter that the Army had suddenly reclassified him and that he would probably be drafted within weeks, February 17, 1966*

Islam

If I hadn't become a Muslim, I wouldn't be who I am today.

—*USA Today*, *December 10, 1999*

I am proud to be a Muslim. Islam has made me feel like a free man.

—The Washington Post, June 9, 1964
Comment made on June 8 as he prepared
to visit the holy city of Mecca during his
first trip to Africa

Islam is the truth and the light.

—The Washington Post, February 28, 1964
At his training camp on February 27,
explaining to reporters why he
became a Muslim

Jack Johnson

Take out the interracial love stuff and Jackson Johnson is the original me.

—*Life* magazine, October 25, 1968
Ali's comments after viewing the play
The Great White Hope, *starring*
James Earl Jones as Jack Johnson

Jokes

Muhammad Ali: What did Lincoln say after being drunk for three days?

Rupert Murdoch: I don't know. What?

Muhammad Ali: I freed the who?

> —*The New York Times,* September 16, 2000
> *Ali and Murdoch at the Rosehill Garden*
> *race track in Sydney, Australia, on*
> *September 14, 2000*

Ali: Superman don't need no seat belt.

Stewardess: Superman don't need no airplane, either.

—*Aggie Daily,* December 15, 2000
Witty flight attendant's reply to Ali when
he offered a clever response to pilot's
order to buckle his seat belt

Fan: What happened to your rope-a-dope defense on Saturday when you got knocked down by Jimmy Ellis?

Ali: I tripped over a left hook.

—*The Washington Post,* April 26, 1976

Student: Who was your toughest opponent?
Ali: My first wife.

—The Washington Post, April 23, 1976
Quip made during a visit to Skyline
Elementary School in Washington

—◆◆◆—

Howard Cosell: Ali clearly isn't the same fighter he was 10 years ago.

Ali: Well, Howard, I just talked to your wife and she says you're not the same man you were even two years ago!

—Comment made on camera on October
30, 1974, as Cosell predicted that Ali would
lose his fight against George Foreman in
Zaire because Foreman was a much
younger fighter

Justice

I think it's a disgrace for people of our stature to only gather $100,000 to capture the killer.

—◆—

There's got to be a Hereafter . . . Then you will pay in hell for eternity.

—Associated Press, May 9, 1981
Ali's comment was made at a press conference
in Atlanta, known for its wealthy African-American
upper middle class, about the reluctance of that
community to put up more reward money to
capture the people responsible for the Atlanta
Child Murders. More than 26 children were
killed. Ali donated $400,000 to the fund.

King

I am the king of the world!

—The Washington Post, February 26, 1964
After beating Sonny Liston for the
heavyweight boxing championship
on February 25, 1964

Last Fight

Dundee told me: "Go out and hit him, go out and hit him." So I said: "You go out and hit him. I'm tired."

—The New York Times, December 11, 1981
After losing the last fight of his career
against Trevor Berbick

Leadership

I could make millions if I led my people the wrong way, to something I know is wrong. So now I have to make a decision. Step into a billion dollars and denounce my people or step into poverty and teach them the truth.

—The Gazette (Montreal), May 20, 2000
Ali made this comment in 1967 when he
was prevented from earning a living as
a boxer by those who resented his
affiliation with the Black Muslims.

Legacy

I'd like to be remembered as a black man who won the heavyweight title and who was humorous and who treated everyone right. As a man who never looked down on those who looked up to him and who helped as many of his people as he could—financially and also in their fight for freedom, justice, and equality.

—Playboy *magazine, 1975*

Life's Purpose

The sun has a purpose. The moon has a purpose. The snow has a purpose. Cows have a purpose. You were born for a purpose. You have to find your purpose.

> —*Ali's advice to children during a visit*
> *to Our Children's Foundation Inc.*
> *in Harlem in 1990*

All of my boxing, all of my running around, all of my publicity were just the start of my life. Now my life is really starting. Fighting racism, fighting injustice, fighting illiteracy, fighting poverty—using this face the world knows so well and going out and fighting for truth.

—*Louisville* magazine, April 1, 2001

I don't know what it was, but I always felt I was born to do something for my people. Eight years old, ten years old; I'd walk out of my house at two in the morning and look at the sky for an angel or a revelation or God telling me what to do. I never got an answer. I'd look at the stars and wait for a voice, but I never heard anything.

—*Sports Illustrated* magazine, January 13, 1992

You lose nothing when you fight for a cause. . . . In my mind, the losers are those who don't have a cause they care about.

—*The Washington Post,* April 2, 1972

I set a goal for myself, to demonstrate to other people what can be done. People tell me not to fight, but they are at the foot of the wall of knowledge and I am at the top. My horizon is greater than theirs.

*—**The New York Times,** November 29, 1981*
Explaining why he was reluctant to retire,
which he believed would mean an end
to his international audience

Service to others is the rent I pay for my room here on Earth.

*—**The Washington Post,** May 15, 1977*
Explaining to South American journalists
why he gave others so much of his
time and money

There's Billy Graham on my left, preaching Christianity. There's a noted rabbi on my right. There's Reverend Ike. There's Wallace Muhammad. All of us preaching [about] our gods, like ponds and streams and rivers and lakes all going down to the ocean. That's why I keep fighting. I'm spreading Islam.

— The New York Times, November 29, 1981
On what life would be like when he
became a minister

Love

Love is a net where hearts are caught like fish.

*—Muhammad Ali's favorite inscription
when signing autographs*

Malcolm X

Malcolm was very intelligent, with a good sense of humor, a wise man. When he talked, he held me spellbound for hours.

—*Muhammad Ali in Perspective*
by Thomas Hauser

You just don't buck the Honorable Elijah Muhammad.

> —*Ali's explanation of why he suddenly severed his friendship with Malcolm X in May 1964. The two had planned to go to Africa together, but Malcolm was suspended from the Nation of Islam for defying an order from the founder of the sect, Elijah Muhammad.*

Maturity

The man who views the world at fifty the same as he did at twenty has wasted thirty years of his life.

—*Playboy* magazine, 1975

Name Change

I don't have to go to court to change it. I'm Muhammad Ali by Almighty God, Allah. . . . I sign my checks Muhammad Ali and they're good.

> *—**The Washington Post,** February 11, 1967*
> *When asked whether he had filed papers*
> *in court to legally change his name*

Changing my name was one of the most important things that happened to me in my life. It freed me from the identity given to my family by slave masters.

—*The Sun-Sentinel* (Fort Lauderdale), July 20, 1997

Unlike many celebrities, Ali lets nothing and no one stand between him and his fans. When he visited this high school in an economically depressed area of Washington, D.C., teachers and students of both sexes rushed in to get a hug; some had to settle for a simple touch.
Photo by Fred Sweets/*The Washington Post* (© 1983). Reprinted with permission.

Ali suppresses a laugh after telling a joke at a 1987 press conference in Washington.
Photo by Bill Snead/*The Washington Post* (© 1987). Reprinted with permission.

In the late 1980s, long after his glory days in the ring were over, Ali continued to have magnetic appeal. Ali gladly complies as children thrust their pens and paper inside his limousine for an autograph.

Photo by Dayna Smith/*The Washington Post* (© 1986). Reprinted with permission.

Ali announces after a 1977 prefight weigh-in that he is contributing $200,000 to buy tickets for distribution to underprivileged people in Washington.
Photo by Richard Darcey/*The Washington Post* (© 1977). Reprinted with permission.

Muhammad Ali and Joe Frazier horse around at the grand opening of Ali's new rotisserie chicken restaurant in Silver Spring, Maryland.
Photo by Keith Jenkins/*The Washington Post* (© 1994). Reprinted with permission.

The father of nine biological and adopted children, Ali plays with the child of one of his fans during a visit to Skyline Elementary School in Maryland.
Photo by Ellsworth Davis/*The Washington Post* (© 1976). Reprinted with permission.

Actor Marlon Brando stands at ringside during a boxing exhibition in Washington to raise money for Native American charitable organizations.

Photo by James A. Parcell/*The Washington Post*** (© 1978). Reprinted with permission.**

Ali takes a break from a rigorous workout at his Deer Lake, Pennsylvania, training camp in January 1974.

Photo By Richard Darcey/*The Washington Post* (© 1974). Reprinted with permission.

During his appearance at the Touchdown Club Luncheon in 1974, Ali predicts disaster for challenger George Foreman.

Photo by Leigh H. Mosley/*The Washington Post* (© 1974). Reprinted with permission.

Soviet Ambassador Anatoly Dobrynin hugs Ali during a visit to the Russian Embassy in Washington, where Ali accepted an invitation to visit Russia.

Photo by Joel Richardson/*The Washington Post* (© 1978). Reprinted with permission.

President Gerald R. Ford was the first American president to invite a much appreciative Ali to the White House. Ali had complained before the invitation that he was one of the few celebrities who had never been invited.

Photo by Bob Burchette/*The Washington Post* (© 1976). Reprinted with permission.

Always proud of his African heritage, Ali admires the embroidered robe and cap given him by Liberian Muslims in Monrovia in September 1980.

Photo by Leon Dash/
***The Washington Post* (© 1980).**
Reprinted with permission.

The champ works up a sweat during a boxing exhibition in April 1976.
Photo by James A. Parcell/
***The Washington Post* (© 1976).**
Reprinted with permission.

*A master of publicity, Ali feigns anger and offers challenger Ken Norton a "knuckle sandwich"
during a prefight meeting at the National Press Club.*
Photo by Richard Darcey/*The Washington Post* (© 1976). Reprinted with permission.

Massachusetts Senator Ted Kennedy chats with Muhammad Ali and his brother, Rahaman, during a reception in Ali's honor at the Senate Office Building.
Photo by Joe Heiberger/*The Washington Post* (© 1974). Reprinted with permission.

Ali is surrounded by several key players in his boxing career at this 1976 weigh-in: trainer Angelo Dundee and boxing promoter Don King stands behind Ali. Ali's only sibling, Rahaman, is the man in the fez to King's right.

Photo by Charles Del Vecchio/*The Washington Post* (© 1976). Reprinted with permission.

Ali demonstrates his "rope-a-dope" technique during a fight against Jimmy Young.
Photo by Bill Snead/*The Washington Post* (© 1976). Reprinted with permission.

Mr. Tooth Decay doesn't stand a chance against Ali at the mock battle in the shadow of the Washington Monument.

Photo by Lucian Perkins/*The Washington Post* (© 1979). Reprinted with permission.

Ali has befriended more heads of state than any other American over his career, that has lasted five decades. Here Prince Salman Bin Abdul Aziz of Saudi Arabia greets him.

Photo by Harry Naltchayan/The Washington Post (© 1989). Reprinted with permission.

When friends need help, they know that they can count on Ali. Ali came to Washington in 1984 to celebrate the grand opening of a Champ Chocolate Chip Cookies store in hard-pressed southeast Washington. His friend Ali Khan owned the store.

Photo by Joel Richardson/The Washington Post (© 1984). Reprinted with permission.

One of the traits that make Ali such an endearing figure is his desire to convert enemies to friends. Despite the Reagan administration's negative image among African Americans, and Senator Strom Thurmond's early career as a strict segregationist, Ali readily met with Thurmond (right) and U.S. Attorney General Edwin M. Meese (in front of Ronald Reagan's photo) in June 1988 during the appointment of Ali's friend Stephen Saltzburg as deputy assistant attorney general.

Photo by Harry Naltchayan/*The Washington Post* (© 1988). Reprinted with permission.

A real hero: Ali hugs a distraught young man after persuading him not to jump from the ninth floor of a Los Angeles building on January 19, 1981.

Associated Press photo (© 1981).

Old Fighters

I don't want to be one of those old fighters with a flat nose saying "duh-duh-duh" before a fight.

*—The New York Times, December 13, 1981,
On why he planned to retire after his
embarrassing defeat by Trevor Berbick in
the Bahamas on December 12, 1981*

Olympic Torch

My left hand was shaking because of
Parkinson's, my right hand was shaking from fear.
Somehow, between the two of them, I got the
thing lit.

> —*The New York Times,* September 16, 2000
> *On his lighting of the Olympic flame*
> *at the 1996 Games in Atlanta,*
> *which he called "scary as hell"*

Parkinson's Disease

What I have suffered physically was worth what I've accomplished in life. A man who is not courageous enough to take risks will never accomplish anything in life.

—News conference, October 1984

People think I'm suffering. People thought I was suffering when they wouldn't let me box during the Vietnam War, too. . . . I want my health back, but I'm not suffering.

—*Sports Illustrated* magazine,
November 15, 1989

———◇———

It would be bad if I had a disease that was contagious. Then I couldn't play with children and hug people all over the world.

—*The Ottawa Citizen,* July 14, 1991

Patriotism

If America was attacked and some foreign force was prowling the streets and shooting, naturally I'd fight. I'm on the side of America, not them, because I'm fighting for myself, my children, and my people. Whatever foreigners would come in, if they saw some black people with rifles, I'm sure they'd start shooting. So, yeah, I'd fight if America was attacked.

—*Playboy* magazine, 1964

Prayer

Most people don't pray until they're in trouble. When people need help, they pray a lot. But after they get what they want, they slow down. If a man takes five showers a day, his body will be clean. Praying five times a day helps clean [the] mind.

—*The Ottawa Citizen, July 14, 1991*

Prognostications

I thought I was through with all that business after I won the title. But my millions of fans won't leave me alone.

—The Washington Post, October 7, 1964
On why he resumed predicting the
outcome of his fights after swearing
off the practice in 1962

Proselytizing

If I just hand out pamphlets, most people would throw them away. But if I sign each one and put the person's name on it, people will keep them and read what the pamphlets say.

—*The Ottawa Citizen,* July 14, 1991

Punch Power

I'm gonna hit this man so hard it'll jar his kin folks in Africa.

—The Washington Post, August 22, 1978
Referring to his upcoming bout with Leon Spinks

Quran

To those who are charitable to others, [God] bestows handsome rewards.

—*The Washington Post,* September 16, 1975
Paraphrasing one of his favorite passages
from the Holy Quran

Religion

A rooster crows only when it sees the light. Put him in the dark and he'll never crow. I have seen the light and I'm crowing.

—The Washington Post, February 28, 1964
In Miami at his training camp, Ali was
explaining why he was admitting that
he had joined the Nation of Islam.

What is all the commotion about? Nobody asks other [boxers] about their religion. But now that I am the champion, I am the king, so it seems the world is all shook up about what I believe.

—◆◆◆—

You call it the Black Muslims, I don't. This is the name that has been given to us by the press. The real name is Islam. That means peace.

—Press conference, February 27, 1964,
confirming his membership in the
Nation of Islam

Retirement

Do I look like I'm ready to retire?

*—The Washington Post, September 17, 1978
After he defeated twenty-five-year-old
Leon Spinks in spectacular fashion.
At thirty-six, Ali was one of the
oldest heavyweight boxers in history.*

I won't miss fighting; fighting will miss me.

—The Washington Post, April 12, 1979

Riddle (Ali's)

That is a question that will forever remain unanswered.

—*The Washington Post,* November 10, 1966
On whether he could take a punch

Running

Running is the source of my stamina. Early in my career I learned to run until I'm tired, then run more after that. The running I do before the fatigue and pain is just the introduction. The real conditioning begins when the pain comes in; then it's time to start pushing. And after that I count every mile as extra strength and stamina—the reserve tank. What counts in the ring is what you can do after you're tired.

—*The Greatest: My Own Story*

Salesmanship

People can't stand a blowhard, but they'll always listen to him.

> —*Commenting in 1964 on his technique for selling tickets. He would brag so much that people who despised him attended his fights because they didn't want to miss seeing him lose.*

There are 16,000 seats in the Convention Hall at Miami Beach, and they cost an average of $76 apiece and they'll all be sold. With the [closed-circuit] theater television, this will be a $7 million fight. I built all that with my big mouth. I should shut up?

—February 6, 1964, at his training camp in Miami

People love to be tricked. They love to be mystified, to see ghosts. We spent $2 billion to get one rock off the moon, and now we won't be satisfied until we get to Mars. And then somebody will say: "I wonder what's on Jupiter?" That's why I'm so good. With my gimmicks, my predictions, I get them riled up to buy tickets.

—*The Washington Post, May 15, 1977*

Self-Confidence

I've never let anyone talk me into not believing in myself.

—*Success* magazine, June 1998

Shah of Iran

He's [Shah Mohammad Reza Pahlavi] their man. We're harboring a thief, and that's wrong.

> —*Associated Press,* November 11, 1979
> *Ali argued that the shah should have been extradited, and he blamed the 1979 hostage crisis, in which 444 Americans were held, on America's coddling of the shah.*

Source of Strength

Three years out of action may have weakened me, but I knew my real strength came from all the Judge Aarons and their faith in me. And I knew I'd soon be stronger than I was before.

—The Greatest: My Own Story
Reflecting on his first conversation
with Judge Aaron, an African-American
war veteran who was castrated by the
Ku Klux Klan

Success

If you want to succeed in business, you have to be true to yourself [and] not compromise your values.

—Success magazine, June 1998

Taxes

It's called the "Joe Louis Law." Before I get paid, they take everything.

—*The Washington Post,* February 24, 1976
Commenting on the high rate of his personal
taxes and alluding to Louis, who made
millions during his career but was always
indebted to the Internal Revenue Service

Time

Father Time caught up with me. I'm finished. I've got to face the facts. For the first time, I could feel that I'm forty years old.

—**The New York Times,** *December 13, 1981*
After losing the fight to Trevor Berbick
in Nassau

Time Travel

The time when Christ was 33, so I could see if he really got up from the grave. Or maybe I'd go back to the time of Cleopatra, before Marc Antony got tight with her. I'd try to hit on her first.

—*Newsweek* magazine, September 29, 1975
*On what time he would like to go
back to, if possible*

Uniqueness

I'm the only man in history who became famous under two names.

—Muhammad Ali in Perspective
by Thomas Hauser

I'm the only boxer in history [whom] people asked [for opinions] like a senator.

—The New York Times Magazine,
May 28, 1967

I'm the only guy who can talk up a $10 million fight in one hour.

—*The Washington Post,* *May 4, 1965*

Vietnam

I'm a member of the Nation of Islam, and we don't have any wars unless they're declared by Allah Himself. I don't have a personal quarrel with those Vietcongs.

—The Washington Post, February 22, 1966

Everybody jumps on me about Vietnam because I say the same things that Senator Fulbright said and Wayne Morse said and Adam Clayton Powell, but the newspapers only pick on me, one poor ex-slave.

—The Washington Post, March 29, 1966

I don't have anything against the Vietcong; no Vietcong ever called me nigger.

—*Muhammad Ali in Perspective*
by Thomas Hauser

Every day, [soldiers] die in Vietnam for nothing. I might as well die here for something.

—*The New York Times Magazine,*
May 28, 1967

Wars

Wars on nations are fought to change maps; wars on poverty are fought to map change.

—*The Washington Post,* March 14, 1975

Wealth

Money and riches don't mean anything to me. I don't care about being a rich individual. I'm not living for glory or for fame. All this is doomed for destruction. You have it today; tomorrow it's gone. I have bigger plans than that.

—*The Washington Post, June 8, 1965*

This country respects only money and winning. So I mesmerize you all with this foolishness—my poetry and predictions and TV shows and sixteen-room mansions. Then you'll listen when I say what I mean.

> *—Explaining why he spent so much time seeking publicity, Ali told fans at a book signing in Washington in 1975 that he was merely setting the stage for his real purpose in life—spreading Islam.*

Weight

Some people can eat and not gain weight, but if I just look at food, my belly gets bigger.

—*Playboy* magazine, 1975

White House

like this place so much that I might go after
your job.

*—To President Gerald R. Ford during a
visit to the White House in 1976*

Winning

Everybody loves me now. My name is magic.

*—**Newsweek** magazine, March 9, 1964*
Reflecting on his new popularity after
taking the heavyweight title from Liston

[A] prizefight is like a war: The real part is
won or lost somewhere far away from witnesses,
behind the lines, in the gym, and out here on the
road long before I dance under those lights.

*—**The Greatest: My Own Story***

I always find a way [to win] when the money is on the table, when the people are in the arena, when the [protective boxing] headgears are off, when the pressure is on.

—*The Washington Post,* September 17, 1978
*Responding to boxing analysts who had
long criticized his poor performance in
training bouts with sparring partners*

Women

When a man can control his life, his physical needs, his lower self, he elevates himself. The downfall of so many great men is that they haven't been able to control their appetite for women.

—*Playboy* magazine, 1964

Even to have one woman around here [in my entourage] wouldn't be right. People would think bad things . . . It's not in our nature to sit around looking at women and not lust after them . . . That would even start a good man thinking wrong, being in a comfortable room with a woman.

—The Washington Post, March 20, 1976

———◆◇◆———

A lot of women rule their men . . . No real man could let himself be ruled by a woman. They nag and they try to push him around. But if he lets her, then he's not the man. She's the man.

—The Washington Post, March 20, 1976

Zaire

This is my home.

—*The Jacksonville Free Press,* April 9, 1997
*On why he accepted an offer from Joseph
Mobutu to fight in Zaire. Ali added that he
wanted to show the world "that Africans
are not natives from a Tarzan movie."*

Verbal Sparring: Ali and Boxing

Ali was perhaps the first heavyweight boxer who tried to defeat his opponents before ever stepping into the ring with them. He did everything he could think of to undermine his opponent's confidence in the days leading up to the fight, from belittling their personal appearance to pulling his big red bus into their driveways with horns honking and bullhorns blasting just before sunrise. He called it "psychological warfare," a strange choice of words given his disdain for psychological testing and war. Many of his opponents fell right into his trap by revealing their anger toward Ali during press conferences. Although some challengers tried to dismiss Ali's poetic predictions about their imminent battles, almost all of them found it difficult to maintain their composure when reporters jokingly reminded them of the sing-song ditties Ali had penned to dishonor them.

Ali on Archie Moore

Moore has been living on the fat of the land,
Now it's time for his pension plan.
Don't block the aisle and don't block the door,
You all may go home after round four.

—*The Washington Post,* *October 14, 1962*

Moore on Ali

When another fighter told Moore that Clay was "outspoken," Moore retorted, "By whom?"

Note: Ali defeated Moore in round four of their bout.

Ali on George Chuvalo

If I get mad [at Chuvalo's tendency to fight dirty], the fight will be over real quick.

—The Washington Post, March 28, 1966
Ali discussing Chuvalo's tendencies to
fight dirty (by hitting below the belt, for
instance) at his training camp in Toronto
on March 27, 1966

Chuvalo on Ali

Don't bother me when I'm working. I'll give you my autograph later.

—*The Washington Post,* January 20, 1966
*To Ali after he showed up at Chuvalo's
camp to observe him spar*

Note: Ali defeated Chuvalo on March 29, 1966.

Ali on Jack Dempsey

I can box one hundred percent better than Tunney and I hit harder than Dempsey.

—*The Washington Post,* November 9, 1964

Dempsey on Ali

Liston is rugged, and this Clay kid is not. . . .
I'd have to say Clay's biggest drawback is his lack
of experience. What's he had, seventeen fights?
I had almost two hundred fights before I was ready
for my first title bout. . . . Clay is still a novice, but
it's not his fault. Money is the reason managers
and promoters push a young kid into the slaughter
pen today.

> —*The Washington Post,* July 11, 1963
> *Dempsey was interviewed in Miami as he*
> *left the funeral of Jack Hearns, the trainer*
> *who successfully guided him to the*
> *heavyweight championship.*

Ali on Sonny Liston

They say Sonny Liston was great, but he must fall for me in eight.

—The Washington Post, October 14, 1962
After Liston defeated Floyd Patterson

Liston is going to be the first Negro to go into space—I'm going to put him there.

Liston will be so scared that he'll leave half his fight in the dressing room. He would rather run through Hell in a gasoline sport coat than fight me again.

—Reply to reporters in Miami on February 18, 1964, who asked him about a possible rematch

Liston on Ali

It could have been worse. It could have happened to me.

—The Washington Post, November 15, 1964
When asked what he thought about his rematch
being canceled due to Ali's hernia operation

The only way Clay can hurt me is by not showing up.

—The Washington Post, January 28, 1964

Note: Ali defeated Liston on February 25, 1964,
with a TKO in the seventh round.

Ali on Joe Louis

What's this about Joe Louis beating me? Slow-moving shuffling Joe Louis beat me? He may hit hard, but that don't mean nothing if you can't find nothing to hit.

—*Muhammad Ali in Perspective*
by *Thomas Hauser*

Louis on Ali

He's got to be kidding! He can't be that bad!

—*The Washington Post,* February 21, 1964
Joe "Brown Bomber" Louis made this
comment on February 20, 1964, after
observing Ali spar for several rounds in
preparation for his first fight with Liston.

Ali on Floyd Patterson

I'm showing you good boxing. You'd be the first to condemn me for killing him cruelly. He has beautiful children and I wouldn't want to hurt him just for the pleasure of the audience. . . . I know I would have hurt him if I hit him.

—*The Washington Post,* January 21, 1966
Explaining why he decided to "carry"
Patterson for six rounds during their fight
on November 22, 1965

Patterson on Ali

I never fought anyone who moved as well as he did. Of all the heavyweight champions, he stands out as far as that's concerned. . . . When we fought . . . there was a certain amount of bad feeling between us. . . . Then, maybe ten years ago when I was a commissioner for the New York State Athletic Commission, I visited his training camp and got to know him better. . . . I was surprised at how much I liked him. He was a nice guy.

—Muhammad Ali in Perspective
by Thomas Hauser

Ali on Rocky Marciano

What was Rocky like? He had once been a loyal admirer of Sonny Liston and had picked Liston to beat me. After I twice destroyed Sonny he became one of my staunchest supporters. Rocky was quiet, peaceful, humble, not cocky or boastful. . . . I lay no blame on him for the outcome of our phony computer fight. He probably had no more knowledge of how it would be finally decided that I did.

—The Greatest: My Own Story

Marciano on Ali

There is nothing around to touch him. He is so good he can make you fight his fight. He may be the fastest ever. He is so alert [that] you can't get a good shot at his chin and he is always moving away when he does get hit. You can't pin him against the ropes.

—Comment made after Ali defeated Floyd Patterson in November 1965. Marciano helped Patterson train for the fight.

Ali on Jimmy Young

A man like Young, you have to lay on him, walk with him—basically, walking and talking, like "Come on, sucker, let's see you get a punch through my defense." If he tries, he'll punch himself out.

—The Washington Post, April 29, 1976

Young on Ali

Why don't you just shut up? People have been hearing your stuff for twelve years . . . but okay, go ahead. You've only got five more weeks to be champion.

—The Washington Post, March 24, 1976

Note: Ali defeated Young on April 30, 1976.

Ali on Brian London

You have to give him credit. He put up a fight for one and a half rounds.

—*The Washington Post,* August 7, 1966

138

London on Ali

He's as fast as greased lightning, the fastest
I've ever seen. He punches faster than a flyweight,
moves faster than a lightweight. But you sure
know you've been hit by a heavyweight. Oh yes,
he's the greatest all right.

> —*The Washington Post,* August 7, 1966
> *Ali knocked London out in third round on*
> *August 6, 1966, in London. London had*
> *been bragging for weeks about what a*
> *dreadful fighter Ali was.*

Ali on Karl Mildenberger

That man was hurt real bad.

—*The Washington Post,* August 8, 1966
*Ali made this statement after telling
reporters that he probably had fractured his
hand on Mildenberger's head in the third
round. Ali had refused to predict the round
that he would end the fight, telling the
media that he was "finished predicting."*

Mildenberger on Ali

Negro boxers always have trouble with my southpaw style. They're instinctive people and find it hard to adapt themselves to a different stance.

—*The Washington Post, September 4, 1966*

Ali on Henry Cooper

covered up when Cooper's eye first split.
I was hoping the referee would stop it. I was
frightened when I saw blood that bad. My religion
doesn't allow me to hurt somebody bad.

—The Washington Post, May 23, 1966
Ali and Cooper both agreed that the referee
was correct in stopping the fight after Ali
opened a deep gash under Cooper's right eye.

142

Cooper on Ali

I am dying to get into the ring with Clay again. If a slow merchant like Chuvalo can catch him with left hooks, then I can. And if I catch him, he won't get up.

—*The Washington Post,* *April 17, 1966*

Ali on George Foreman

You're the champ and I'm beating you up.

—*The Washington Post,* October 31, 1974
*To Foreman during their fight in Zaire
on October 30, 1974*

Foreman on Ali

I'm the best fighter that ever lived. I'm the greatest. I'm the Number One Wonder of the World. I'm going to knock him out in three rounds.

—*The Washington Post,* October 25, 1974
Foreman was imitating Ali before their October 30 date.

Note: Ali knocked Foreman out in the eighth round.

Ali on Joe Frazier (first fight)

I really won . . . but the political beliefs were against me and he got the decision. The next time there will be no doubt for I will knock him out.

—*The Washington Post,* September 17, 1971

Frazier on Ali (rematch)

I don't like Clay and that's honest. He gives you the same old jive. I've got five times the class he has. I've been training since October and I'm going to come out smokin'.

— *The Washington Post,* *January 15, 1974*

Note: Ali beat Frazier on March 8, 1974.

Ali on Leon Spinks (rematch)

I have told the world I will beat this vampire if I stay out of the clinches and don't let him bite me on the neck.

> —*The Washington Post,* September 14, 1978
> He called Spinks "the Vampire," he said,
> "because he doesn't have his [two] front
> teeth and you can see his fangs."

Note: Ali defeated Spinks on September 14.

Spinks on Ali

He's still the greatest; I'm just the latest.

—*After beating Ali in their first match,*
February 1978

Final Bell:
Everybody's a Critic

The odd thing is that Clay is dangerous to under-estimate. He took all the bad habits possible into the ring against Liston at Miami Beach and rose above them spectacularly to stop the big man who was supposed to be invincible. Everything was supposed to be wrong with Clay going into that fight, but everything came out right.

—Shirley Povich, **The Washington Post,**
May 20, 1964
Povich was a long time critic of Ali
whose opinions influenced other
sportswriters and bettors.

Angelo Dundee on Ali

Ali is not great yet, but he is going to be the best heavyweight of them all. He already has the best left hand that I've ever seen. . . . Yes, better than Joe Louis, Tommy Loughran, or Sonny Liston, who had a strong jab.

—*The Washington Post,* November 21, 1965

Howard Cosell on Ali

Muhammad Ali is a figure transcendental to sport. He's important to the history of this country because his entire life is an index to the bigotry lodged deep within the wellspring of this nation and its people. The only other person to come out of sports who might be as important as Ali was Jackie Roosevelt Robinson.

—*Muhammad Ali in Perspective*
by Thomas Hauser

Elijah Muhammad on Ali

Two thousand years from now people will still know your name and tell of what you did.

—The New York Times Magazine,
May 28, 1967

Howard Patterson
(former bodyguard) on Ali

Whenever he saw someone old or sick or in trouble, Ali always wanted to help them. He'd say: "Who knows? Someday I might be that way."

—*Sports Illustrated* magazine, April 25, 1988

Harry Brill-Edwards on Ali

I suppose what impressed me most about Ali was the way he cared for everyone. He had a kind gesture for absolutely every person he saw. . . . I told my family when I got home: "I've always known that Ali was a super sportsman, but during those hours that we were together, inside that enormous body, I saw an angel."

—The Ottawa Citizen, July 14, 1991
Brill-Edwards was one of fifteen hostages
released into the custody of Muhammad
Ali in November 1990 by anti-American
Iraqi rebels.

Reggie Jackson on Ali

Do you have any idea what Ali meant to black people? He was the leader of a nation, the leader of Black America. As a young black, at times I was ashamed of my color; I was ashamed of my hair. And Ali made me proud. I'm just as happy being black now as somebody else is being white, and Ali was part of that growing process. . . . Do you understand what it did for Black Americans to know that the most physically gifted, possibly the most handsome, and one of the most charismatic men in the world was black? Ali helped raise black people in this country out of mental slavery. The entire experience of being black changed for millions of people because of Ali.

—www.houseofboxing.com, May 21, 2001
Comment made to Thomas Hauser

Leon Gast on Ali

I believe, in the truest sense of the word, that Muhammad Ali is a hero. His presence explodes off the screen. He is a hero in comparison with the so-called icons of today. All athletes today are looking for is a good endorsement deal. There are so few real heroes. Is there anyone that you can really look up to?

Note: Gast is the director of the documentary *When We Were Kings*.

Wilfrid Sheed on Ali

His picture hangs in African mud huts where they don't always know what he does for a living; Arab kings lay villas on him like Kleenex; he is the toast of England, the fastest route to an argument in America, and altogether the noisiest piece of work since Telstar made possible the global shriek.

—*The Hartford Courant,* January 17, 1992

Bibliography

BOOKS

Ali, Hana. *More Than a Hero: Muhammad Ali's Life Lessons Presented Through His Daughter's Eyes* (New York: Pocket Books, 2000).

Ali, Muhammad with Richard Durham. *The Greatest: My Own Story* (New York: Random House, 1975).

Ali, Muhammad with Thomas Hauser. *Healings* (New York: Collins Publishers, 1996).

——— . *Muhammad Ali: His Life and Times* (New York: Simon & Schuster, 1991).

Bingham, Howard L. and Max Wallace. *Muhammad Ali's Greatest Fight: Cassius Clay vs. the United States of America* (New York: M. Evans, 2000).

Early, Gerald. *The Muhammad Ali Reader* (New York: HarperCollins, 1998).

Hauser, Thomas. *Muhammad Ali in Perspective* (New York: Collins Publishers, 1996).

Mailer, Norman. *The Fight* (Boston: Little, Brown, 1975).

Marquesee, Mike. *Redemption Song: Muhammad Ali and the Spirit of the Sixties* (London: Verso, 1999).

Miller, Davis. *The Tao of Muhammad Ali* (New York: Warner Books, 1996).

Olsen, Jack. *Black Is Best: The Riddle of Cassius Clay* (New York: Putnam, 1967).

Pacheco, Ferdie. *Fight Doctor* (New York: Simon & Schuster, 1977).

——— . *A View from the Corner* (New York: Carol Publishing Group, 1992).

Remnick, David. *King of the World: Muhammad Ali and the Rise of an American Hero* (New York: Random House, 1998).

Schulberg, Bud. *Loser and Still Champion: Muhammad Ali* (Garden City, N.Y.: Doubleday, 1972).

PERIODICALS

"Ali Seeks $50 Million from U.S. for Vietnam War Rift," *JET* magazine, January 13, 1986, p. 17.

Axthelm, Pete. "A Fight to Remember," *Newsweek* magazine, October 13, 1975, p. 72.

Bonventre, P. "An Ex-champ's Days—Not the Greatest," *People* magazine, March 12, 1984, p. 109.

Deford, Frank. "The Best of Friends," *Sports Illustrated* magazine, July 13, 1998, p. 82.

Edwards, Audrey and Erica Lumiere. "Stand by Your Man: Lonnie Ali, the Wife of Former Heavyweight Boxing Champion Muhammad Ali," *Ladies' Home Journal,* October 1996, p. 112.

Hauser, Thomas. "Ghosts of Manila," www.houseofboxing.com/Hauser/hauser05-21-01.asp/, May 21, 2001.

Hiltbrand, D. "Float Like a Butterfly, Sting Like a Bee . . . The Man for All Seasons as Muhammad Ali," *TV Guide,* May 6–12, 1989, p. 41–2.

Kram, Mark. "Shadowboxer; Muhammad Ali," *Playboy* magazine, January 1984, p. 178.

McKenzie, Michael. "Muhammad Ali: Lessons From 'The Greatest,'" *Success* magazine, June 1998, p. 68–70.

Miller, D. "My Dinner with Ali," *Sport* magazine, May 1989, p. 70.

"Muhammad Ali and Joe Frazier Agree to End Thirty Years of Quarreling," *JET* magazine, April 2, 2001, p. 48.

"Muhammad Ali and Wife Lonnie Share Secret to Their Happy Marriage," *JET* magazine, December 6, 1999, p. 32.

Nack, William. "The Fight's Over, Joe," *Sports Illustrated* magazine, September 30, 1996, p. 52.

—— . "Young Cassius," *Sports Illustrated* magazine, January 13, 1992, p. 70.

"New Ali Center CEO Believes $80 Million Goal Can Be Met," *Business First* magazine, November 3, 2000, p. 8.

"Odessa Lee Grady Clay, 77, Mother of Boxing Legend Muhammad Ali, Dies," *JET* magazine, September 12, 1994, p. 54.

Plimpton, George. "The Greatest: Muhammad Ali," *Time* magazine, June 14, 1999, p. 98.

Ransom, Lou. "Ali Is Now Fifty! Won Title Three Times, Married Four Wives, Has Nine Children and Millions of Fans," *JET* magazine, February 10, 1992, p. 54.

Recio, M. E. "Will the Ali Car Ever Come Out of Its Corner?" *BusinessWeek* magazine, January 12, 1987, p. 133.

Rogin, Gilbert. "A Champ Like No Other; Recollections of Ali When He Really Was the Greatest," *Sports Illustrated* magazine, April 25, 1988, p. 112.

Smith, Gary. "Ali and His Entourage," *Sports Illustrated* magazine, April 25, 1988, p. 47.

—— . "A Celebration of Muhammad Ali," *Sports Illustrated* magazine, November 15, 1989, p. 215.

Strasser, Steven. "Muhammad Ali, Diplomat," *Newsweek* magazine, February 18, 1980, p. 58.

Talese, Gay. "Boxing Fidel; Meeting Between Fidel Castro and Muhammad Ali," *Esquire* magazine, September, 1996, p. 138.

Young, D. "Muhammad Ali," *Sport* magazine, December 1986, p. 18.